Peas and Prose

Soph Truepenny

BookLeaf Publishing

Presentation by *BookLeaf Publishing*

Web: www.bookleafpub.com

E-mail: info@bookleafpub.com

ISBN: 9789357441261

First edition 2023

To my younger self, who loved life fiercely, who viewed every year as an improvement on the last, who thought it couldn't get any better, who tried things in the face of a fear of failure - I am reaching for that part of you now.

To my present self, who threw themself into this to tease confidence from a timid typist, clicking away to write prose in a candlelit room, who knew this would challenge the perfectionist still supervising her mind.

To my future self, who I know will read this and cringe, but who I hope valued the experience.

I am starting to believe in you.

ACKNOWLEDGEMENT

Thank you for loving me and letting me share
this with you.

PREFACE

This collection isn't a life story, it isn't defining, it isn't my worst work, it isn't my best either. It is a fragment of a fragment. It is some of the words I wish I could've said, and some I will inevitably grow to wish I hadn't said. It is self-fulfilling, and self-destructive and incomplete in its entirety. It is the parts I guard and the parts I bare.

One

There was once a girl who lived in a sunny
home, a palace full of joy and dreams.
An unruly baby, born with her heart put into a
cage, not on her sleeve.

Each night her king and queen would tuck her
in, and as she slept she grew, and as she grew
she learned and as she learned she smiled.

And she ran into the world, and played and
laughed. And the kingdom taught her, to be and
to try... and to love, and to cry.

Her thoughts grew wild, and far from the box
they had given her to contain them in. And she
exercised this, roaming the gardens of mind. Not
afraid of the thorns, or a petal left behind.

But as her heart grew too, and she learned to
listen, it ached. It told a different story,
something scary and new.

For the people shamed a heart like hers. They
were subtle but relentless. Even from herself,
she kept it hidden. Secret, precious.

And this heart in its cage stopped the flowers
from growing. The paths were cut short - she
was lost and unknowing.

With clouds overhead, she didn't like this new
world. A constant frown, unsettled, the soil
disturbed.

And to calm the unrest, she ventured out, and
then in. She fought to blossom again, and to
dance and to sing.

Because for the first time she saw people with
hearts like hers. People who loved openly
without fear, in spite of the slurs.

She knew now, she was one of the lucky ones,
understanding with age,
it was nothing wrong with her heart, and
everything wrong with the cage.

Burn at the well

The devil himself, makes a monster of the
humble unmade bed,
and the untaken shower, the unwritten essay.
He steals from time, crumpling the afternoon in
a sweating palm
like a crisp white letter, resigned to a floor of
mistakes.

And he returns when the day sleeps. He returns
to accompany the night,
to entertain and to humiliate.
The creaks of the bed laugh a mocking cry.
Turn and turn, and watch the clock run until
dawn.
Hear then a different cry, and burn at the well for
your toast.

He blames me, he blames a rudeness, he blames
an inconsiderate.
He blames this heart that beats for the forgotten,
and the way it flits
between the given ways of living.
I try in vain to tease moments of gratitude from
what shakes and keeps me awake.

But I find I am restless of my own doing
anyway.

What, when I am gone, will they think of the
jigsaws I have left?
I fight in these moments, a reluctant resilience
balancing lightly in my favour.
Time on his side now, but the light of the
morning sun on mine.

The architect and the engineer

nothing ever ends
in such a profound matter
as we say it does

the northern lights
are more vivid
in our minds

and when it's over we write prose
and sculpt poems
to cast a memory
in gold

but you love me like sunlight and butter
and tea
and honey
you hug me like nothing hurts

like you would die a million times
like I am already golden

Poem 4

Forgotten words knock at my mind
Words I had intended to share
The rainbow wasn't bright today
But it was there

Sit with me

She collected the petrol they'd left for her
And doused it over the hope I'd been building
And there she set fire to it
And I watched through glass eyes.

Sit with me, join me in warming our hands on
this fire
On the hope they burn and let us watch
God knows you need it too
But for your sake too, let me grieve.

Let me grieve without being force fed
Watch the flames dance in my eyes without
trying to put it out.
Let me be responsible for building it
Again.
I am carrying the world and more wood will be
the straw.

The embers are almost ashes. Let me let them
go, please,
or let me go too.

She is not a poet

She plays with words like a child with Lego. She builds castles with a rhythm like a song, each word dripping with meaning and light and life and painting with rich oils and dark pastels.

She takes a breath and steps back from her work. But it doesn't carry the weight she holds.

She sees her life in broken photos and moonlight where there should be sun. She twists her senses so she can hear the light and taste the sound, her body still, her mind pulsing, creation and gravity fighting under the surface like fusion in a star. And her chest folds with each breath, but she makes it back in time. In time for the elevator doors to open. And she's sat in the field, pulling at the clovers and tickling the soil.

Ahead, the unmarked graves rest in their three. She strains to hear the cry of the fox, and the reply of the dog.

The night seems to echo outside of reach. But she types in the dirt, and finds herself in the

place of forgotten moments. A candle stares and
follows her into the squeezing room. Thick
carpet threads scratch at her heels and she opens
the box on the mantle.

So, it plays, night after night in that corner in
that room, in another for a while, and another
then back at number thirty-three. A black book
of mundane days stamped thick in ink.

The breath calls her back to the grass, her mind
on the hell in her rising chest. In her falling
chest. Still folding.

So, she rearranges her bones and settles her skin,
into a better posture. She prods at her mind and
moulds reason into a blank slate.

Two

And now she knew, she felt she should share this heart.
She wanted to, too.

But here she lay, numb and a head spinning from the events of the day, unable to move, or concentrate for a while...

She thought of the things she would do, before this pain.
She would play games, and cycle, and read, and live. Truly live.

Even now, with the gardens growing again, they felt bare, like she couldn't see them in colour, or smell the scents they gave.
Though the paths all connected, and how to cultivate it, she knew,
there she stood, frozen in the heat.

There were some things she didn't know.

She had lost trust in the people, they didn't have all the answers.

And for the first time, she looked for a gate.
What existed outside the garden? Could she
leave?

For the weather was too unpredictable here. She
craved something like nothing.
But on the green stretched

So she sat down, and she picked at the grass.
She felt the blades tug at her fingertips

Fireplace ghost

The night is less dark when you give it time
Life is less heavy when you put it down for a
while
I sit at the monument
Memory of to whom it is dedicated is long
forgotten
At least for us
And now it represents times of communal tears
Long midnight conversations
Meeting halfway
Photo shoots
And that time
When the snails seemed to spawn
In their hundreds

Tonight, though
I watch the stars blink
And blink back new asterisms
Dot to dot
The windows are mostly dark
But bright lights lead the gravel way
With the red brick towers
Far but familiar

I pick out the trees
But they don't yet have names
And I sit at the centre of a
Green maze
That's not truly a maze
We were kids really
Taking photos under the late blossom
Whipping gowns
Double steps to
Catch up

Maybe we're still kids
Maybe we're still haunted
By the ghost of J— H—
In the gardens
After dark

Maybe I am her
A stooped figure
Indistinguishable
From the same lumpy trunks and wide bushes
Those eyes saw too
And my hands start to freeze

So in I retreat
Back out of the maze
By the hedges and the bright lights' haze
And up the apples and pears

An old coat

Going home is like being forced into an old coat
that no longer fits.

I squeeze into it, uncomfortable, and I don't
recognise myself. But they don't recognise me
without it.

And all the trips are so fleeting there isn't time
for me to take it off. Show them who I am now,
how I act and what I like.

Maybe I play with the fabric, and they notice it's
altered my posture, but press on without a word.

Or I start to tell a story, but the zip catches and
suddenly lies tumble from my lips to protect this
old image.

And they don't seem to have changed at all, but
maybe they're hiding in small layers too.

New future

15

Christmas chocolate
Wrappers tumble
From your pocket
When you try to find your key
To the home and heart
We share

We fill our boots
With clumsy love and you dance
With the butterflies you leave
In my tummy
As we crunch through
Snow and wonder
If this is Sapphos'
Temperate dream

We slip inside
And light candles
And to you I feed
Sweet laughter
On the carpet
We haven't hoovered

A Sunday romance
You teach me to knit

Warm hands over warm hands
And I teach you to skate
Laughing hands over wobbly hands
Over ice
Over each other
And you might teach me Greek
And I might break it

And much as we try
To protect and hold it still
Time slips free and with candle smoke
Leaves through the window

We live her life again, us two
Or three
And don't worry
We remember you
Though we have lost it too,
Time

And our comfort is still
A walk in the cold, bitter
And a hot chocolate homecoming, sweet
And each others words
Like poetry
To the ears
Like sweet christmas chocolates
To the lips

Peas

a pain in my chest
in my knee
in my hands
pain in inaction
in knowing
and not doing

rubbish on the pavement
a beer bottle at the bottom
of the earth
red lines on sentenced trees
rang tans sentenced too
as they reach for sweet fruits

puddles where there should be worms
on the concrete
and cut grass
by humans not herbivores
mismanagement
and inaction
in knowing
and not doing

and a pain in my heart
bricks in my head

that I fashioned into a wall
every chance I got
and bricks I added
and knew I should break
but knowing is not doing
and action I did not

the peas under my mattress
that keep me up

Do they lie?

Who are we if we shuffle our pages
And pluck some, and dog ear memories
And let them scribble in our edges
And ink mark their criticisms and
Compliments tattooing moments
Building and circling phrases
But with tea that drips unsweetened
Between the lines and smudges
Words we've yet to write
We dream in shreds of others
Sentences scraping reality deciding
Where symbols end and faces start
And do we really know these,
Or do they lie?

Jane and the girl

Jane was slow and gentle. Unrecognised and underappreciated. At first, the girl was frustrated - she wanted her job done and couldn't stop to think. Too tightly bound to function, surely.

But Jane saw the girl with a new pair of eyes, no reputation, no history. Only she saw the girl how she was. Then. Not clouded by image.

The girl was learning to lead, and learning to manage, and learning to care.
But Jane was there, every day with a smile and an anecdote. Jane told her stories, hands clutching the cloth in her lap, smile on her face. And together they would grumble at the crumbs or the noise, a hearty and healing rant often shared.

For Jane never judged - she was open and curious, in ways the girl hadn't seen before. And Jane remembered, always.

But the girl would leave, back to her classes and her peers, and Jane to her life too. The daily check-ins a stable thread, a life tether.

And though wildly different, and generations apart, the pair would laugh together, and cared for the other's stories and lives. And the girl learned more from Jane than she did from her classes. She learned even if she chose to ignore it, that life is about relationships, and connections, and common ground. And that slow is good. Slow is measured, and constructive, and at peace.

Before she knew it, the years had slipped through her fingers. The girl, no longer really a girl.

The girl had grown to care, and grown to love. But had to move on. And the world swept her up, and to Jane she spoke not, for a number of months. She often dreamed of the things she would say, the postcards she would send, and the stories she might be able to tell.

But Jane left too. When Jane was gone, the girl broke, stood in place. She hadn't seen the tether, or appreciated it, until it was no more.

And the people didn't see their friendship, they didn't see the time or the joy or the shared disgust. Oblivious. They missed out.

The girl didn't know Jane's family, she didn't
know her life outside of that crazy room. She
wondered if she knew Jane at all.
But she did, and she grieved alone. For
relationships like theirs were uncommon among
the people - and who can console the unknown?

And still, the girl wonders, if enough people
knew Jane as she felt she knew her. If she meant
as much to Jane as Jane did to her. She often
dreams of the things she would say, the stories
she would tell if Jane had been given another
day.

Three

As she read, her eyes welled. She had forgotten the calm this used to bring.

Her head was so stuffed she wondered how she had once had the clarity to write any such words. Yet they brought back some of that clarity. Some of that peace on a wobbly timeline.

A string of band names. A bucket of pills. A cluster of poems.

She thought of how 'the girl' in the verses had changed. How maybe she wasn't a girl anymore. But not in that way. She had grown of course, but that familiar uncomfortable had again become just that, familiar.

She thought of the books she had read, and how they had framed her new ideas. And how she might share her words. That felt too far for just now.

And although she didn't feel so stuck as she had as a 'girl', she couldn't fly yet either. Stuck on the threshold of a well-trodden cage.

Me for now

five syllables they gave me

a perfect rhythm

I cannot repeat

one that won prizes and dripped smiles

a 'pleasure to teach' child

five syllables or six

a sturdy chime

of two who care

a gift to me

from a love, a cat and three towns

third time lucky

and 'my little sister'

but lately it's been slipping

six five four

I lose my childhood and more in one breath

lose or let go

two letters in essence

gifting me to them

We had met twice before I fell in love with you

I feel like I have grown up with you
In a way only mirrored by my home
You're bursting with life
But you hide a maze in your soul
False, monumental and cold
But it is here I felt most close to you
And the stars you worship

Like me, you love the sunsets
You praise and frame them
I have always wondered if you paint them, too

And you sing at dusk and dawn
But let us rest
And I have always wondered
If you hold up the sky for us here, too

And when the day faded you took to the night
It is here I know I have to leave you
Relationships like this don't last forever
But I will keep the photos

The photos of when you loved me too

Sensitive

Everyone thinks she is not the sensitive one. But I see she is sensitive in ways they know not. Sensitive to the way their faces change in her attempt to broach a new subject. A brick. Sensitive to the way they stay. A brick. Sensitive to the way they describe each other, less perfect, and more real but painful to the ear. Another brick. And she is sensitive to the half-truths they tell about what they think of people like her.

It's up to her to tease their inherited ideas and ideals from between their hand-me-down lines.

Though let her be reminded, that alone as she may be in this clip of time, her ancestors felt this too. The same ancestors that let these bricks be passed to her, were themselves burdened.

So it's her hands that build the wall around her fire. It's her hands which shield them from the light that burns within her, shields them from when it wobbles, shields them from when it threatens to burn down villages. But it is their bricks. Bricks they didn't know they gave to her. Didn't know they were handed themselves.

She is sensitive but they forced her not to show
it to them.

paint my words

if it happens
paint my words in blood
on the floors of those who walk
over my rights
as I write

if it happens
paint the sky with my words
in fire or in light-up drones
blind them while they rest
where I could not

if it happens while you're away
take your time
but put my body where the others say
put my body where the people who killed me
have to see it
limp

if it happens before we succeed
make it known I will not
rest in peace
there is no peace when I cannot live
when I cannot live and be acknowledged
as I am

if it happens before I tell you
and you find out from a friend
take it well
I didn't mean for it to end

Christmas

While the children are young, we make-believe at Christmas, we talk of magic and write to a mystical figure who brings bundles of toys and has flying reindeer to help him. We leave out food as thanks, and the adults keep the secret. The adults make-believe too.

We spend weeks searching for special things to give to show we care. We'll fret and we'll worry. And we'll hide them in shiny paper and pile them under the glowing pine tree that resides in the window for the month. Balls of silver and beads and this year tiny characters in tiny hats perch on its branches.

For two dozen days we count down with a chocolate behind some foil and a small cardboard door. In this time, guests to the house are greeted with a small pie and hot spicy wine, they complement the decorations, and the gifts are delivered, and cards with Christmas pictures and scribbled greetings frame the windows.

And all the people smile on Christmas morning. We eat chocolates for breakfast, and pancakes for elevensies, After, the paper is shed and the presents are loved.

We make good food - hearty seasonal vegetables, staple potatoes, someone pours over the roast turkey for days. And we pile them all high and smother it in gravy. And we sit around a decorated table and pull at card parcels until they crack open. We wear the tissue crowns folded up inside, and tell bad jokes and roll eyes, and laugh at the clippers or mini cards that flew at the wall. And we eat pudding, sticky toffee here, with sticky sauce and sticky smiles. And we make a mess of the tablecloth and drink each other's wine and remark that we forgot the peas, or the sprouts. And around the table the family are grateful to have each other, blood and chosen, here and away.

And we tire, and retire to the lounge. In dribs and drabs, half-drunk drinks at our feet and swaddled in blankets, we dose in front of the screen, pretending to listen to the monarch and their speech.

And the pup reminds the people of fresh air, so they wrap themselves in layers of wool and feathers, and lace their boots with good grip, slipper socks poking out the top. The young ones walk in their pyjamas. The air outside is thick and cold. They see their breath as they talk. And they see other families through other windows, with other traditions. And other families out, all sharing well wishes and smiles, and a comment on the weather no doubt.

And upon return, we eat again, a mother's spread, to the sound of her claim there's not enough. And some read new books, and some rest, and some continue to eat. Some watch stories acted out on the screen, taken to other worlds, or put into other shoes. And some cry on this happy day, a reminder of past days and the people left in them. And some light candles, and some pray. I think of the people who made it this way.

And as the visitors leave, the family mumble up the stairs that we forgot to take any photos, but it's okay, because we enjoyed our day.

You won't always

I am scared, blind down, no light peeks
I lie in my fear of the thoughts and of the pain
And nothing works, not alone anyway
Sleep creeps with an unknown face, and a
broken promise
How do I access these future memories of a life
I haven't lived?
Of a life I thought I might never allow myself to
live?
Is it a true paradox, or a self-fulfilling prophecy,
that my failure to imagine prevents
continuation?
No, but the paradox festers in me.

Preach, but don't sow. Don't reap. Be real, but
not like that. We're here for you, but not when
you do that. How are you, but don't tell us the
truth.

You won't always be afraid. You won't always
be lonely. You won't always feel pain.

You won't always.

Skeletons

35

maybe we find skeletons under the stairs
in the church that raised us
and we wonder if those are souls who couldn't
make it
out

we wonder whether
we can squeeze into the world they made for
themselves
and if we lift our pens, we ask
what is art?

perhaps it will be read, or trodden on, in a studio
by a clumsy grandmother
or perhaps it will be thrown away by the chance
art critic cleaner
who answers

not this